Patrick Henry

History Maker Bios

Catherine A. Welch

BARNES & NOBLE

NEW YORK

TABLE OF CONTENTS

INTRODUCTION

Patrick Henry was born in Virginia on May 29, 1736. There was no United States of America then. Virginia was one of thirteen British colonies.

But Patrick and many colonists wanted Great Britain's control of the colonies to end completely. Patrick Henry was a fiery speaker for freedom. He spread the spirit of revolution throughout the colonies. His daring words stirred the colonists to fight for independence.

This is his story.

1

THE SPIRIT TO LEAD

Patrick Henry grew up on a plantation in Virginia. This large farm had many buildings and fields, as well as forests and streams. Patrick loved roaming the countryside with his two brothers and seven sisters.

Patrick was a spirited boy. At times, he liked to stir up fun and trouble. Sometimes he and his friends took canoe rides. Patrick liked to tip over the canoe, soaking his friends.

Other spirited people lived in Great Britain's colonies in America too. Patrick saw new preachers come and stir up the people. The official church in Virginia and some other colonies was the Anglican Church, also called the Church of England. But many colonists were unhappy with the Anglican Church. Some Anglican ministers did not seem to care about the people. These colonists did not want to follow the Church of England. They wanted greater religious freedom.

Virginia had been a colony of Great Britain since the 1600s.

This desire for freedom made some colonists turn to the new preachers, who were Presbyterians. Like Anglicans, Presbyterians were Christians. But they followed Christianity in a different way. Patrick and his mother heard the new preachers give fiery sermons. "Save your souls!" the preachers cried out.

Sarah, Patrick's mother, liked their new words of faith. She became a Presbyterian. Sometimes she took Patrick to hear the Reverend Samuel Davies preach. Patrick thought Davies was a great speaker. Patrick watched wide-eyed as Davies sometimes boomed out a single word, "Arise!" On the way home, Patrick's mother asked him to retell the sermons.

Church was a very important part of colonial life. For many people, it was the only time they saw their friends.

Patrick's father, John Henry, studied at King's College in Scotland. It was founded in 1495.

But Patrick did not follow the new faith. He went to church with his father, John. John had grown up in Scotland and attended King's College there. John was well educated. Patrick learned to read and write in a nearby school. But his father taught him mathematics, Latin, history, and some Greek.

Patrick and his father went to an Episcopal church. (The Episcopal Church was connected to the Church of England.) They heard Patrick's uncle, Parson Patrick Henry, give quiet sermons about faith, honesty, and good works. Many men at this church were local leaders. Perhaps Patrick saw himself as a leader one day.

Patrick and his brother owned a general store like this one. People would come from miles away to buy food and cloth.

When Patrick was fourteen, his family moved to a new home in Virginia's backcountry. The few settlers there were uneducated farmers and woodsmen. Patrick loved hunting and fishing near his home.

Patrick's family could not afford to send him to college. When he was fifteen, he began working in a country store. A year later, he and his brother William set up their own general store. But the business failed.

At eighteen, Patrick had no job. But he did have some good news. He married Sarah Shelton in 1754. As a wedding gift, Sarah's father gave the couple six slaves and the three-hundred-acre Pine Slash Farm.

Patrick worked in the tobacco fields with the slaves. He cleared the land and pressed seeds into the soil. He weeded and harvested crops. It was rough, sweaty work. Crops grew poorly during a summer drought and early fall frost.

Patrick and his wife, Sarah, received Pine Slash Farm as a wedding present.

Patrick and his family lived in Hanover Tavern. It was both a tavern and an inn.

In 1755, when Patrick was nineteen years old, he and Sarah had their first child. They named her Martha. But bad times were coming. In 1757 fire destroyed the Henrys' house. Patrick struggled to support Sarah, Martha, and their new baby. For a while, they lived in an inn owned by Sarah's father. There, Patrick gladly helped with the guests at the inn's tavern. He enjoyed listening to their conversations.

Some of the guests were lawyers. Patrick listened to them boast about cases they had won. Lawyers were becoming important leaders in the colonies. Patrick wondered if he should become a lawyer. He was smart, liked people, and was a good talker.

During the Christmas of 1759, Patrick thought about his future. He took his family to his parents' house. But he spent most of the time at the home of Colonel Nathaniel West Dandridge. The colonel was wealthy and knew important people.

The colonel's parties were lively. There was wine, punch, laughing, and dancing. Patrick enjoyed simple country life. But he also enjoyed the social life of the colony's most important people. Yes, he decided. He could see himself as a lawyer. He would study for the law exam.

PATRICK AND THOMAS

Patrick Henry met Thomas Jefferson at the Dandridge plantation. Thomas was seven years younger than Patrick. At first, Thomas did not like Patrick's coarse country manners. But Thomas had fun watching Patrick fiddle and dance. They got to know each other and shared ideas. Jefferson later became the third president of the United States.

2 THE POWER OF WORDS

Eager to start his law career, Patrick borrowed two law books. He may also have watched trials at the county courthouse. Then in April 1760, he traveled fifty muddy miles to Williamsburg by horseback.

Patrick must have been excited. This was his first visit to Williamsburg, which was then the colony's capital. There, the colony's best lawyers questioned him for hours. They did not like his country clothes and manners. He did not look like a very bright fellow. But Patrick was a quick thinker. He passed the exam.

Patrick began his law career with small cases. Then, in 1763, Patrick got his first big case—the Parson's Cause. The case was about the Anglican ministers' salaries. The ministers represented the official church of England. They were loyal to the king. But they were paid by the colonies.

Actors show what Williamsburg might have been like when Patrick was alive.

Ever since 1696, the ministers had earned a certain amount of tobacco each year. This meant their salaries went up and down with the changing price of tobacco. In 1755, tobacco crops had been very small, which made tobacco prices very high.

Virginia's General Assembly passed a new law. It let colonists use money to pay ministers. They would pay the ministers two cents for each pound of their tobacco. But tobacco was selling for much more than two cents per pound. The ministers wanted a larger payment.

Tobacco was a valuable crop in the Virginia colonies.

Patrick defends the colonial taxpayers during the Parson's Cause trial.

The ministers protested to Great Britain. Finally, the Reverend James Maury won a law case to get more pay. Now the court had to decide how much to pay him. Patrick would be the lawyer for the colonial taxpayers.

At the courthouse, Patrick stood up to speak. At first, he fumbled for words. The clergy looked at this big red-haired fellow and laughed. They were sure Patrick would lose the case.

But Patrick kept speaking. A hush fell over the room. Words stormed out of Patrick's mouth. The colonists could not afford to pay more, he said. The ministers were greedy! They would "snatch . . . the last hoe-cake" from the people.

Patrick knew the court must pay Maury some amount. But he told jurors to award him only one farthing—less than a penny. And they did.

Patrick won the case. The taxpayers were overjoyed. They carried him on their shoulders around the courtyard.

News of Patrick's bold speech spread throughout the colony. His words got people thinking. An ocean separated the colonies from Great Britain. Why should they listen to the king? Did the king know their needs or care about them?

George III was the king of Great Britain. Many colonists thought he was too far away to understand them.

In 1765, Patrick was elected to Virginia's House of Burgesses. This group of leaders discussed local matters. Most of these men were wealthy tobacco planters. They wore silks and laces. Patrick looked out of place in his shabby clothes. But he had big ideas.

Patrick knew colonists were angry about the Stamp Act. British lawmakers had passed this tax law. Colonists would have to pay a tax on nearly all printed materials. The tax would even be on playing cards.

GOVERNING THE COLONIES

In Virginia and many colonies, Great Britain appointed a governor and governor's council. They made sure the king's laws were obeyed. In Virginia, the landowners elected members to the House of Burgesses. The governor's council and house made up Virginia's General Assembly. The assembly made laws about local matters. But the governor had to approve the laws.

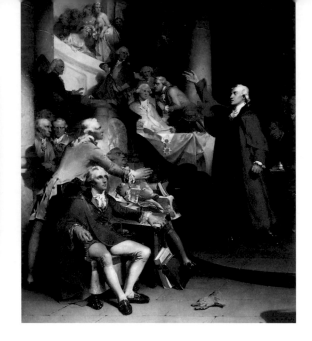

Twenty-nine-year-old Patrick tells the House of Burgesses, "If this be treason, make the most of it."

In May 1765, Patrick was ready to fight the Stamp Act. He entered the House of Burgesses with a list of reasons against the tax. He declared that only the colonists had the right to tax themselves. The king's lawmakers could not tax them. That was against the colonists' rights.

Patrick's words sparked an angry debate. Virginia was the oldest colony. It was the most loyal to Great Britain. During Patrick's speech, several house members thought he was being disloyal to the king. They shouted "Treason!" Patrick replied, "If *this* be treason, make the most of it."

Thomas Jefferson—another rising leader in Virginia—watched the debate from the door. He later said that Patrick was the greatest speaker he had ever heard. In the end, the House of Burgesses agreed with most of Patrick's ideas. Virginia was the first colony to oppose the Stamp Act.

News of Patrick's speech spread. Soon other colonies joined Virginia in protest. People formed secret groups called Sons of Liberty to fight the Stamp Act. They urged colonists not to buy any British goods. People began to fight for their rights. Patrick was pleased.

Soon British merchants lost money. In March 1766, King George III ended the tax.

The Stamp Act angered many colonists. Some of them gathered in the streets and burned stamps in protest.

For several years, Patrick kept busy with his law work. As his family grew, he bought Scotchtown Plantation. It had almost one thousand acres. The land had perfect soil for growing tobacco and wheat. It also had a cabin for Patrick's law offices.

Patrick still owned several slaves. He knew life would be much harder without slaves. But he thought slavery was evil. He believed that someday slavery in the colonies would end.

People can still visit Patrick's Scotchtown Plantation in Virginia.

Most wealthy colonial men wore clothes like the ones Patrick is wearing in this portrait.

By 1769, Patrick's law business had grown. He took major crime cases in Williamsburg and appeared in front of the colony's highest judges. He dressed like a wealthy man. He wore a black suit and wig. Patrick finally looked like the important person he was.

3 SPIRIT OF REVOLUTION

By 1773, Patrick's father died, and his wife became mentally ill. Sarah could no longer care for their six children or even herself. A slave cared for Sarah in their home. Others helped with the children.

Meanwhile, the spirit of protest was growing. Patrick was happy about that. He wanted the colonies to communicate with one another. He helped create a group to share ideas with other colonies. In the spring, the group talked about not paying the British tax on tea.

In September 1774, a Continental Congress of colonial leaders met in Philadelphia. Congress members would talk about what to do next. Was it time to go to war against Great Britain?

Patrick was excited to meet the leaders from other colonies. Many were lawyers and skilled at debating. When he first spoke at the Congress, other members whispered excitedly to one another. "Who is it?" they asked.

THE BOSTON TEA PARTY

In 1773, the colonies refused to buy British tea because of the tax. But angry colonists wanted to send an even stronger message to the king. On December 16, some colonists dressed as Native Americans. Then they boarded British ships in Boston Harbor and threw the tea overboard. The king got the message. But he responded by shutting down the port. That made things worse for Boston.

Patrick (CENTER FRONT) traveled to the First Continental Congress in Philadelphia.

Some men wanted to share ideas freely. But some did not trust leaders from other colonies. Patrick tried to bring trust into the meeting. He said, "I am not a Virginian, but an American."

In the end, the Congress decided not to go to war yet. Patrick returned to his plantation. He found that it was hard to get news there. Would the colonies ever be willing to fight Great Britain? he wondered.

Later in the fall, British officials banned the colonies from buying gunpowder and arms. The king did not want colonists using these against British troops.

Meanwhile, Patrick's family problems grew worse. In February 1775, Patrick's wife died, but there was no time to grieve. In March, Patrick hurried to another meeting. The Second Virginia Convention brought together leaders of the colony. Patrick urged them to prepare for war.

But some still felt some love and duty to Great Britain. They hoped to settle things peacefully. A fierce debate followed.

Patrick (STANDING LEFT) debates issues at the Second Virginia Convention.

Then Patrick rose to speak. "There is no longer any room for hope," he said. "If we wish to be free . . . we must fight."

Some leaders thought the colonies were too weak to fight. But Patrick pressed on. "I know not what course others may take," he said. Then he paused and flung out his arms. "But as for me—give me liberty, or give me death." He ended by plunging an imaginary dagger in his heart.

Patrick (STANDING LEFT) delivers his great speech on the rights of the colonies to the Virginia Assembly.

A poster asks Americans to join the fight for independence.

The room was silent for several minutes. Then the debate went on. Finally, the men voted to prepare for war. Patrick led a committee with Jefferson and others. They made plans for arming the colony.

Each county needed men to volunteer for a militia. Members of the militia must be ready to fight. Many Virginia militiamen began wearing shirts with Patrick's words, "Liberty or Death."

Colonial soldiers fire on British troops at Lexington. This battle was the first one of the American Revolution.

In April 1775, the British tried to seize colonists' weapons stored in Concord, Massachusetts. But the militia battled them at Lexington and Concord. They forced British troops back to Boston. The American Revolution had begun.

In May, Patrick and other colonial leaders met for a Second Continental Congress in Philadelphia. By June 16, they agreed to create a Continental army. Congress members named Virginia's George Washington the army's commander in chief.

Patrick helped Washington organize the army. Men from farms, frontiers, and towns joined the army. These men, along with the militia, would fight for freedom!

4 ARMING THE COLONIES

In August 1775, Patrick became colonel of the First Virginia Regiment. He became commander in chief of the Virginia militia. Patrick was a bold, patriotic leader. Men rushed to join his militia.

But Patrick had no military experience. Some powerful military men did not want Patrick in charge of the Virginia forces. Patrick wanted to lead troops in battle, but he resigned in February 1776. He decided he could be more helpful off the battlefield.

Later that spring, Patrick and other Virginia leaders met for another Virginia Convention. At the meeting, Patrick said the colonies must declare independence as soon as possible. In the end, his fellow Virginians agreed. In May 1776, convention members decided that Virginia would declare itself independent. And they decided that at the next Continental Congress, the colony's representative would vote for all the colonies to be independent.

In June, convention members agreed on Virginia's first state constitution. They also elected Patrick Henry to be the first governor of the independent state of Virginia.

Patrick Henry helped lead Virginia in the fight for independence.

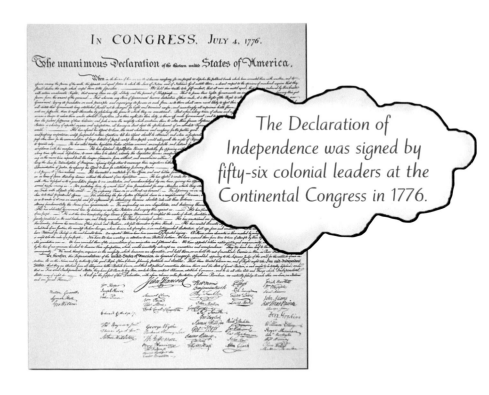

The Declaration of Independence was signed by fifty-six colonial leaders at the Continental Congress in 1776.

On July 4, 1776, the leaders at the Continental Congress agreed on a Declaration of Independence. This bold statement said the colonies were free from Great Britain. But they still had to fight to win that freedom.

As governor, Patrick faced new challenges. He made decisions about military supplies and salaries. The troops needed gunpowder, weapons, and warm wool clothing for winter.

An officer trains troops during a cold winter at Valley Forge, Pennsylvania.

By September 1776, the Continental army was taking shape. But the soldiers still needed to be trained. They had to learn how to advance and retreat, fire, and reload their guns. Officers had to make sure troops were clean and healthy. There were plenty of things to worry about.

On March 29, 1777, Patrick wrote to General Washington. Patrick worried that not enough men were joining the army. And troops were sick and dying from smallpox.

Meanwhile, Patrick married Dorothea Dandridge. She was twenty-two years old, and Patrick was forty-one. Dorothea helped care for Patrick's children. She also helped him host guests at the Governor's Palace in Williamsburg.

But Patrick still worried about the troops. During the winter, the troops were cold and hungry. Patrick worked hard to send wagons of supplies to the soldiers.

While Patrick was governor, he and his new wife, Dorothea, lived in the Governor's Palace in Williamsburg.

In 1778, Dorothea gave birth to a daughter. The next year, Patrick's time as governor ended. He had served for three years. He and his family left Williamsburg. They moved to a ten-thousand-acre plantation in Henry County, Virginia. This county was named after Patrick. Patrick's plantation supplied corn for the army and food for the horses.

With each passing week, the war came closer to Patrick's doorstep. In 1780, Richmond became Virginia's capital. It seemed safer than Williamsburg. But soon, no place seemed safe from the British.

British troops often destroyed fields and towns as they marched through the colonies.

The British attacked Williamsburg one week and Richmond the next. Patrick worried about his family. He had guards who placed their guns through portholes in the house.

By May 1781, things looked hopeless. Supplies were low, and men refused to join the army. Patrick met with other leaders to talk about the problems. Jefferson had been elected governor, and Patrick urged him to order more militiamen into service.

IMPORTANT ARTICLES

In 1777, the Continental Congress adopted the Articles of Confederation. This document united the colonies under one government. But it did not give the central government many powers. It gave the U.S. Congress the right to declare war and to borrow money from other countries. But the states kept the power to tax the people. In 1781, the articles were accepted by all the states.

But the meeting suddenly ended as British troops stormed into town. Patrick and the others fled for their lives, but the British captured seven men. Then troops destroyed the arms storehouse and attacked one of Jefferson's plantations, burning crops. No one knew how long the war would last.

5 AFTER THE REVOLUTION

On September 3, 1783, Great Britain signed a peace treaty with the United States. The war had finally ended. The United States of America was a free nation at last. Patrick was proud of his new country.

In November, Patrick was elected Virginia's governor again. He was still a popular patriotic leader. He served two more one-year terms as governor.

Meanwhile, Virginians talked about religious freedom and taxes. Some said church should not be tied to government. Taxes should not support any church, they said.

Patrick did not think that anyone should have to follow a specific religion. But he also felt that religion encouraged people to be good citizens. He hoped the Episcopal Church would be the main church.

Many people disagreed. They believed that the state should have nothing at all to do with religion. Through their work, Virginia passed a bill for religious freedom in January 1786. It declared that no one should be forced to follow or support any religion.

James Madison (LEFT) and Thomas Jefferson (RIGHT) believed that religion and government should be separate.

George Washington (STANDING RIGHT) leads the Constitutional Convention in 1787.

Another issue was the Articles of Confederation. Many state leaders wanted to revise this document. Some wanted a stronger central government. In 1787, a Constitutional Convention took place. Patrick did not go. He did not want a stronger government.

Convention members kept the meetings secret. In September, most members approved a new U.S. constitution. But it was not yet the law of the country.

Washington sent a copy of the constitution to Patrick. Patrick still worried about the central government becoming too powerful. So he attended the Virginia Convention of 1788.

Convention delegates discussed the new constitution. Some believed it protected all the rights of the people. Patrick and others disagreed. They wanted to add a bill of rights. Patrick thought the constitution needed some simple language to clearly explain the rights of all citizens.

One by one, nine states accepted the constitution. Then everyone waited to see what Virginia would do. Virginia finally approved it by just a few votes. Patrick had lost his fight to add a bill of rights.

In 1789, George Washington became the first president of the United States. On December 15, 1791, ten amendments—the Bill of Rights—were finally added to the Constitution. Patrick was happy.

THE BILL OF RIGHTS

The First Amendment of the Bill of Rights protects freedom of religion and freedom of speech. These rights were especially important to Patrick Henry.

Patrick spent the last five years of his life at Red Hill plantation in Virginia.

In the new government, Patrick was offered many important jobs. They included senator, chief justice, and secretary of state. But his health had begun to fail.

Patrick spent his remaining years with his family on a large plantation known as Red Hill. On January 15, 1798, Patrick's seventeenth child was born. He died at Red Hill of stomach cancer on June 6, 1799.

As a young man, Patrick Henry struggled to find his place in life. But he finally did. He learned that he had a talent for speaking. He learned that his spirited words could move people to do great things. He was the voice of the Revolution.

TIMELINE

In the year . . .

1752 Patrick became a storekeeper with his brother.

1754 Patrick married Sarah Shelton.

1760 he passed the law exam and became a lawyer.　Age 24

1763 he won his first important legal case, the Parson's Cause.

1765 he gave his famous Stamp Act speech in the Virginia House of Burgesses.　Age 29

1772 he became a member of Virginia's Committee of Correspondence.

1774 he attended the First Continental Congress.　Age 38

1775 his wife Sarah died.
he gave his famous "liberty or death" speech.
he was elected colonel of the First Virginia Regiment and commander in chief of the Virginia militia.

1776 he became the first governor of the independent state of Virginia.　Age 40

1777 he married Dorothea Dandridge.

1785 he was reelected for a fifth term as governor of Virginia.

1788 he was elected to the Virginia House of Delegates and to the Virginia Convention.
he supported adding a bill of rights to the U.S. Constitution.

1799 he died on June 6 at Red Hill in Virginia.　Age 63

LIBERTY OR DEATH?

Patrick Henry is remembered for his "liberty or death" speech. Historians are sure that Patrick gave an exciting speech on March 23, 1775. But they are not sure of the speech's exact words. No one took notes the day of the speech.

Years after Patrick Henry died, William Wirt wrote Patrick Henry's life story. Wirt spoke with people who had known Patrick and heard some of his speeches. From interviews, Wirt pieced together Patrick's famous speech. It was first published in 1816. Wirt found that Patrick's speech probably did end with the words, "Give me liberty, or give me death." And we do know that those words have inspired many people. They stand for the spirit of the American Revolution.

Patrick Henry's speech is one of the most famous of the American Revolution.

FURTHER READING

Day, Larry. *Let It Begin Here!: Lexington and Concord, The First Battles of the American Revolution.* New York: Walker & Company, 2005. Learn more about the beginning of the American Revolutionary War.

Graves, Kerry A. *The Constitution: The Story behind America's Governing Document.* Langhorne, PA: Chelsea House Publishers, 2004. Explore the Constitution!

McPherson, Stephanie Sammartino. *Liberty or Death: A Story about Patrick Henry.* Minneapolis: Carolrhoda, Inc., 2003. Read more about Patrick Henry and his life.

Random, Candice. *George Washington.* Minneapolis: Lerner Publications Company, 2003. Meet one of Patrick's fellow patriots and the United States' first president.

Sherrow, Victoria. *Thomas Jefferson.* Minneapolis: Lerner Publications Company, 2003. Explore the life of Thomas Jefferson, another important leader from Virginia.

Sirvaitis, Karen. *Virginia.* Minneapolis: Lerner Publications Company, 2002. Patrick Henry was Virginia's governor five times. Learn more about his home state.

WEBSITES

Colonial Williamsburg—Kids Zone
http://www.history.org/kids/ Learn more about colonial life at this website.

Red Hill: Patrick Henry National Memorial
http://www.redhill.org This website includes a virtual tour of Red Hill, as well as links to other sites about Patrick Henry.